NATIONS IN CONFLICT
INDIA & PAKISTAN

by CHRIS HUGHES

BLACKBIRCH®
PRESS

THOMSON
—————TM
GALE

San Diego • Detroit • New York • San Francisco • Cleveland • New Haven, Conn. • Waterville, Maine • London • Munich

THOMSON
—————✳—————™
GALE

Photo credits: cover, pages 11, 15, 19, 20, 21, 22, 26, 29, 31, 33, 36, 38, 41, 42 © CORBIS; page 5 (map) © Amy Stirnkorb Design; pages 6-7, 28, 34, 35 © AP Wide World; pages 8, 10 © Blackbirch Press Archives; pages 11, 44 © Corel Corporation; pages 12-13 © Karl Grobl.com; page 16 © Art Resource; page 23 © Library of Congress; page 24 © Hulton Archive;

LIBRARY OF CONGRESS CATALOGING-IN-PUBLICATION DATA

Hughes, Christopher (Christopher A.), 1968-
  India & Pakistan / by Chris Hughes.
    v. cm. — (Nations in conflict)
Includes bibliographical references and index.
Contents: Place, people, past — Political turmoil — India and Pakistan's future.
  ISBN 1-56711-539-X (hardback : alk. paper)
  1. Pakistan—History—Juvenile literature. 2. Pakistan—Foreign relations—India—Juvenile literature. 3. India—Foreign relations—Pakistan—Juvenile literature. [1. Pakistan. 2. Pakistan—Foreign relations—India. 3. India—Foreign relations—Pakistan.]
I. Title: India and Pakistan. II. Title. III. Series.
  DS382.H76 2003
  954.91—dc21   2002015927

CONTENTS

A Region of Strife

In May 1998, the nation of India set off five underground nuclear explosions. Barely two weeks later, India's neighbor Pakistan tested two nuclear devices of its own. The world paid close attention. India and Pakistan were only the sixth and seventh nations ever to admit publicly that they had usable nuclear weapons. Even more frightening was the fact that these two nations, which share an 1,800-mile-long border, had weapons aimed at each other.

India and Pakistan have come to the edge of war mainly because of a long history of religious conflict. India's people are mostly Hindu, whereas Pakistan is made up almost completely of Muslims. For centuries, members of these two religions have opposed each other in and around India. Different beliefs about all aspects of life, from worship to diet, have caused misunderstanding and anger between the two nations, and more than a thousand years of conflict have led to deep distrust.

One major dispute is over the region of Kashmir (called Jammu and Kashmir by India). This region, located in northwestern India and eastern Pakistan, is claimed by both nations. India controls about two-thirds of Kashmir, and Pakistan controls the other third. Fighting in Kashmir

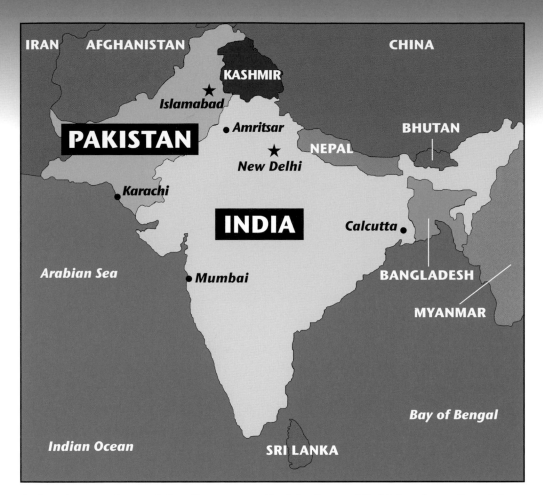

helped cause two of the three wars that India and Pakistan have fought against each other since 1947.

Historically, India and Pakistan were not two separate countries. Until 1947, the entire region was called India. American author Mark Twain once described it as "the cradle of the human race, the birthplace of human speech, the mother of history, the grandmother of legend, and the great grandmother of tradition."[1] The region, located in the southern-most part of Asia, is sometimes called the subcontinent of South Asia.

Besides India and Pakistan, the area includes Nepal, Bangladesh, Bhutan, and the island of Sri Lanka. Combined, these six nations are home to more than 1.3 billion people—more than one-fifth of the world's population. The fact that the two largest and most powerful of these nations are close to war is a crisis that concerns the entire world.

The Indian Agni missile (pictured) can travel over 1,242 miles. The potential for nuclear war between India and Pakistan is a concern that is shared by the rest of the world.

अग्नि II मिसाइल
AGNI II MISSILE

CHAPTER ONE

Place, People, Past

Modern India is the world's seventh largest country in area. It sits on a peninsula that extends from the Himalaya Mountains in the north to the Indian Ocean in the south. India has a wide range of climates and geographical features, including some of the world's highest mountains. The center and south have tropical heat for much of the year, but in the north, the highest elevations can be dangerously cold. The Ganges River runs across the widest part of India's peninsula, and the plains that surround it are fertile and densely populated. The Deccan Plateau makes up the interior of the southern peninsula, and smaller mountain ranges called the Eastern and Western Ghats run along either side of the country. India has several large cities, including Mumbai (Bombay), Calcutta, and Delhi. The capital, New Delhi, was built in the twentieth century next to the much larger city of Delhi.

In Pakistan, the Indus River runs from the northern mountains (which include K2, the second highest peak in the world) to the Arabian Sea. Much of the Indus River Valley is fertile, and many Pakistanis live in or

Calcutta is one of India's largest cities.

The Himalaya Mountains form India's northern border.

near it. Although Islamabad is the nation's capital, Pakistan has several larger cities, including Karachi and Lahore. The Thar Desert lies along part of the border between India and Pakistan.

India and Pakistan are affected by monsoons, or seasonal winds that bring dramatic weather changes. Between March and May, the winds are hot and dry through most of the region, but starting in May or June, they bring torrential rain. This rainy season lasts until September or October. The period from December to February is generally the coolest time of the year.

India's Hindu Culture

The mix of climates and geographical regions has led many different groups of people to settle and develop the land of South Asia over time. The Indus River Valley was the site of one of the world's oldest and largest civilizations—the Indus, or Harappan, civilization, which dates to about 3000 B.C. Hinduism and Indian culture developed sometime later, as described in a book called the Rig Veda, which has been traced back to at least 1500 B.C. The Rig Veda, the oldest religious text still used today, is one of four holy books called Vedas that contain some of the basic concepts of Hinduism, as well as hymns and stories.

Developed over a long period of time, Hinduism is one of the world's most flexible and adaptable faiths. Although several books, including the Rig Veda, explain elements of Hinduism, there is no book that gives a set of fixed rules or commands as the Christian Bible and Muslim Koran do. Although Hindus generally believe in one supreme god, they also have many lesser gods that are often variations of the main god.

Hindus consider cows to be sacred.

Hindus believe in reincarnation, or the soul's journey through many lives as it seeks freedom from the cycle of life, death, and rebirth. Hindus believe that when a person dies, his or her soul enters another being, and continues to do so each time the body dies, until the soul achieves such a high level of enlightenment or understanding that it no longer needs to follow the cycle.

Hindus do not eat beef. They consider cows sacred because of their peaceful, giving nature. Since they believe that all animals have souls, Hindus are often vegetarians, and many practice nonviolence toward people and animals. Buddhism, a religion found mostly in central and east Asia today, and Sikhism, found in the Punjab in northwestern India, were also

---

People use the Ganges River both for transportation and as a source of drinking water.

founded by Hindus. The world's third largest religion after Christianity and Islam, Hinduism does not claim that its ideas are the only path to salvation. It teaches that many paths can lead to the same place.

In India, Hinduism has been both a religion and a way of life. For most of India's history (and even today in some areas), Indians followed a strict caste system—a system of social levels—based on Hinduism. A person is born to a certain level and cannot change his or her status. The four castes are brahmins (priests), kshatriyas (warriors), vaisyas (farmers and merchants), and sudras (servants). Members of a group outside the caste system, sometimes called "untouchables," are below the sudras.

Although the caste system helped keep order in Indian society, it also led to unfair treatment of the people at the lowest levels of society, who were discriminated against by law and by tradition. Poor treatment sometimes caused lower-caste Hindus and untouchables to convert to religions that view all people as equal, such as Islam, and later, Christianity.

Islam in India

Islam is the main religion of Pakistan, and the second largest in India. Islam was brought to India by a series of invaders who crossed over a mountain road called the Khyber Pass, located between the modern nations of Pakistan and Afghanistan. These Muslim invasions began around A.D. 700, although at first, relations between Hindus and Muslims were mostly peaceful and centered around trade. About A.D. 1000, a Muslim army under Mahmud of Ghazni invaded northern India and destroyed Hindu cities and temples. In 1139, another Muslim leader, Muhammad Ghori, conquered the region of Delhi, and beginning around 1200, most of northern and central India was ruled as an Islamic state called the Delhi Sultanate.

Muslims praying in India.

Clashes between Muslims and Hindus became frequent. The Muslim rulers placed high taxes on all non-Muslims and forbade any religious practices that conflicted with Islam. Hindu temples were destroyed, and Hindu cows were killed to feed the Muslims. In some areas, small independent Hindu states remained, but they were heavily taxed by the Muslims and were often attacked.

The Muslims themselves were not always united. As the Delhi Sultanate expanded its rule from northern India into central and southern India, it was attacked by Muslim Mongol armies from northern and central Asia. Around 1525, a Mongol named Babur overthrew the Delhi

Hindus and Muslims worked together under the leadership of Mogul ruler Akbar (center) in the mid-to-late 1500s.

Sultanate. Babur began the Mogul Dynasty, which spread Muslim rule over most of India except the far south. Babur continued to discriminate against Hindus and sometimes used extreme violence. According to one historian, after one of Babur's battles, "triumphal pyramids were raised of the heads of the slain, and on a hillock which overlooked the field of the battle, a tower of skulls was erected."[2]

Babur's grandson, Akbar, later eased the restrictions on Hindus. His Edict of Toleration for All Religions gave non-Muslims the chance to serve in the government and removed some of the heavy taxes the Hindus had borne. Under the rule of Akbar and his grandson, Shah Jahan, both Muslim and Hindu cultures thrived. Hindus and Muslims worked together to advance the empire, and the independent Hindu states were allowed to exist in peace. When Shah Jahan died in 1658, however, his son ended the period of tolerance. In response, Hindus and other non-Muslims rose up against the Moguls, and by 1800, the Mogul Empire was almost completely destroyed.

India Falls Under British Rule

By then, there was a new force in India—Europeans. In 1498, a Portuguese explorer named Vasco da Gama had arrived. The Dutch, French, and British followed the Portuguese, and by 1750, the more powerful British were chasing the other Europeans out of southern India. They wanted to use India as a stopping point for their ships involved in the profitable trade with the Far East, but they soon discovered that India itself had valuable spices and goods.

As the Mogul Empire collapsed, British control expanded. To build their influence over India, the British made treaties with certain local leaders and opposed others. At first, a British trading company called the East India Company controlled India, but as the region's value became clear, the British government took direct control in 1858.

British rule brought about new advances in transportation and communications. Health care and education were also improved, and agricultural production was increased. Some people, however, claimed that the British used India's resources only for the good of England and mistreated the Indian people. The crops they forced the Indians to grow were often dyes and other goods for British factories, instead of food for India. The British passed laws that required Indians to buy clothes from English mills and to pay high taxes for necessities such as salt. The British rulers also made English the primary language for business and politics, and brought Christian missionaries to try to convert both Hindus and Muslims. Any protesters were usually arrested and jailed. To Indians, these acts showed no respect for Indian culture or history.

Resistance to British Rule

In 1885, a group of influential Indian leaders founded the Indian National Congress. This group was made up of both Hindus and Muslims, and its goals were to achieve equal treatment for both Indians and British subjects under British law, and eventually, to gain freedom from England. British leaders tried to divide the congress by telling Muslims that if independence were achieved, the Hindu majority would ignore Muslim concerns. Many Muslims also feared that if Hindus gained control of India, they might take revenge on Muslims for centuries of mistreatment. The British used this fear to undermine the Indian National Congress, and in 1906, the Muslim members withdrew to form the All-India Muslim League. From then on, the British were able to pit the groups against each other by spreading rumors and increasing their mutual distrust. Though both groups stood against British rule, they could not work together.

As resistance to their rule grew, the British made some effort to give the Indians more rights and opportunities. They set up a system that gave Indian leaders some control over health and education. The British still controlled finances, trade, taxation, and the police, though, so the new system did not silence the complaints of most Indians.

In 1919, British soldiers opened fire on a peaceful gathering in the city of Amritsar. Hundreds of Indians were killed and more than a thousand wounded. British general Reginald Dyer, who directed the attack, was later put on trial, and his comments showed that he had little concern for Indian lives. When asked why he opened fire, he declared, "I could have dispersed the crowd without firing, but they would have come back again and laughed."[3] Although Dyer was eventually removed from duty, the so-called Amritsar Massacre further strengthened Indian opposition to British control.

One person in particular had begun to win fame for his stand against

Hindu leader Mohandas Gandhi organized boycotts of British goods. This picture shows one such protest in 1922.

British rule—Mohandas Gandhi. A devout Hindu, Gandhi supported non-violent opposition. He also called for peace between Hindus and Muslims and for an end to mistreatment of untouchables. When many Indians wanted to strike back violently at the British, Gandhi pointed out, "An eye for an eye only makes the whole world blind."[4] Gandhi made use of the fact that there were so many more Indians than British. He organized strikes, marches, and boycotts of English goods, and urged Hindus and Muslims alike to stop cooperating with the British.

HINDU-MUSLIM DIFFERENCES

Hinduism and Islam, the two dominant religions in southern Asia, have a long history of conflict. Some of the conflict has been political, since Muslims ruled much of South Asia from A.D. 1000 through the eighteenth century. Many Muslim rulers tried to force the people to practice Islam, and Hindus usually had fewer rights, higher taxes, and little if any voice in government compared with Muslims. The conflict was more than just political, however. Significant differences between Islam and Hinduism have made it very difficult for the two religions to exist alongside each other.

Most Hindus worship one main god among many lesser gods and

The Jama Masjid mosque in New Delhi is one of the largest in India.

Hindu priests may offer prayers to the rising sun.

spirits, whereas Islam accepts only Allah as the one true god. Hindus often represent their gods with holy statues and pictures, but Muslims are taught that there should be no worship of images. Hindus do not eat beef, because they believe that the cow is a sacred animal that should not be killed. Islam forbids eating pork, because the Koran teaches that the pig is an unclean animal, not fit for humans to eat. The Hindu caste system is another area in which the two religions have opposed each other. Islam teaches that all people are equal, and some Muslim rulers would not allow Hindus to openly follow the caste system.

Living side-by-side in India turned these differences into potential clashes because some practices by one religion were seen as offensive to the other. Centuries of often repressive Muslim rule also brewed resentment.

The divisions between Hindu and Muslim beliefs have led to misunderstandings, oppression, and at times, outright warfare in India.

The British Decide to Withdraw

Eventually, these methods made the British realize that they could not control India forever. Gandhi's demand for nonviolence, even when he and his followers were attacked or jailed, gained him respect and recognition throughout the world. In the 1930s, Great Britain slowly began to grant more independence to India and gave Indian leaders more responsibility over new areas. British leaders did not want the negative attention Gandhi's protests brought to Great Britain, and eventually, they no longer wanted the expense of maintaining control over India. After World War II ended in 1945, England made the decision to free India.

The question of how India would be governed once the British withdrew arose immediately. Since India had a large Hindu majority, any democratic vote would result in a Hindu government. Jawaharlal

In the 1930s, the British government met often to discuss India's independence.

Nehru, a close friend of Gandhi and the leader of the Indian National Congress, seemed to be the best candidate to lead an independent India.

This was not acceptable to India's large Muslim population, however. Although Muslims had fought against British rule, often alongside Hindus, there was still deep distrust between the two groups. Leaders of the Muslim League, especially Muhammad Ali Jinnah, demanded that England separate the Muslims completely from Hindu India.

Jawaharlal Nehru (left) and Mohandas Gandhi (right) both believed that dividing India into two countries would make Hindu and Muslim relations worse.

The Partition

Jinnah pressured England to partition, or split, India into two nations: Hindu India and Islamic Pakistan. (The name Pakistan means "land of the pure" in the Pakistani language of Urdu.) He stated, "We have to fight a double edged battle, one against the Hindu Congress and the British Imperialists. . . . The Muslims demand Pakistan where they could rule according to their own code of life and according to their own cultural growth, traditions and Islamic laws."[5]

Gandhi and Nehru both feared that a division of India into two nations would only make relations between Hindus and Muslims worse. They thought the only way for the two peoples ever to gain understanding was to live together in an independent state. To Muslims, though, "independent state" meant Hindu state. In 1947, over the strong objections of Gandhi and Nehru, Great Britain agreed to the partition. India was given its independence, and Pakistan was created.

CHAPTER TWO
Political Turmoil

According to the partition, Pakistan was to be made up of regions where there was a Muslim majority population. Since that was the case in the northeast and northwest of India, Pakistan consisted of two states, East Pakistan and West Pakistan—but they were separated by 1,000 miles of Hindu-controlled India. There was also another problem. Regardless of which group made up the majority, many Hindus lived in Pakistan and many Muslims lived in India. All those people would have to decide whether to stay where they were and live as part of a minority population, or pack up and move.

Millions of Hindus and Muslims chose to move to their "own" territory. They feared persecution and mistreatment if they stayed where they were in the minority. The ongoing religious friction and the new resentment of those who felt they were forced to leave their homes were made worse by political tensions. Hindus believed that Muslims were stealing Indian land, and Muslims accused Hindus of trying to prevent the establishment of Pakistan. Fights and riots broke out, especially in border areas and in cities where the population was mixed.

In 1947, crowds on the streets of Calcutta celebrated India's independence from Great Britain.

Organization of Two New Nations

After so many years of British control, India followed the British political system when it formed its first government. Nehru, as head of the Congress Party, became India's leader as the constitution was written and a democratic process set up. In Pakistan, the Muslim League chose Jinnah to serve as the governor-general and president of the assembly that was writing Pakistan's constitution.

Even as two new governments were organized and attempted to deal with the conflicts caused by the partition, there were still many unanswered questions. The partition agreement allowed some Indian states that

Jawaharlal Nehru (foreground) was India's first prime minister.

had been partly independent under British rule to choose whether to join India or Pakistan. Most states decided quickly, based on their location and religion, but two states did not. Hyderabad, on India's southeastern coast, had a Muslim ruler but a mostly Hindu population, and it was completely surrounded by India. At first, Hyderabad chose to remain independent. In 1948, however, Indian troops invaded and forced the state to join India.

The Fight for Kashmir

The other state that chose to stay independent was Kashmir. Located in the north, along the border between India and West Pakistan, Kashmir had a Hindu ruler and a population that was mostly Muslim. Although both India and Pakistan initially agreed not to interfere while Kashmir made its decision, Pakistani troops crossed the border in late 1947. Kashmir's Hindu leader asked India for help, and Indian troops arrived to push out the Pakistanis.

Although Indian and Pakistani citizens had been fighting already, this was the first direct military action between the two nations. The conflict raged for 14 months, until the United Nations (UN) negotiated a cease-fire. When the fighting stopped, two-thirds of Kashmir was occupied by India and one-third had fallen under Pakistan's control. The UN called for a popular vote in Kashmir so the people could decide their own future, but that vote never took place. India refused to allow it until Pakistan withdrew from Kashmir. Today, the land of Kashmir is still divided along the 1948 truce line. The Indian section is called Jammu and Kashmir (Jammu is the region just north of Kashmir). The land that lies within Pakistan is called Azad Kashmir, which means "Free Kashmir."

The war in Kashmir and the fighting along the borders claimed as many as one million lives between 1947 and 1948, and tens of millions

In October 2002, a rally was held to promote a free and independent Kashmir. India and Pakistan have been fighting over the right to rule Kashmir since 1947.

of people fled their homes. Despite the fighting, Gandhi attempted to restore the practice of nonviolence. He had some success at first, but in 1948, he was assassinated by Nathuram Godse, a Hindu who believed that Gandhi was too generous to Muslims. The world was shocked at Gandhi's death. Ethiopia's emperor, Haile Selassie, spoke for many when he said, "Gandhi will always be remembered as long as free men and those who love freedom and justice live."[6]

After the cease-fire, both countries took advantage of the peace to focus on their own governments. Muhammad Ali Jinnah died in 1948, and Pakistan's National Assembly, made up mostly of former All-India Muslim League leaders, ruled Pakistan until the constitution was finished in 1956. In India, Nehru's party was victorious in India's first open election in 1950. Nehru became prime minister, and the Congress Party, made up mostly of leaders of the former Indian National Congress, dominated the Indian parliament.

A Second Fight Begins

In 1965, new fighting broke out between India and Pakistan over control of a section of India's northwestern border. Although war was never formally declared, heavy fighting quickly spread into Kashmir and beyond.

Karachi and New Delhi were bombed in air raids. Again, the UN was able to arrange a cease-fire, and both sides promised to withdraw from territory they had taken over in the fighting. A fragile peace was restored.

In addition to the military clash, both countries faced internal problems. Nehru's death in 1964 had taken away India's last founding father. In 1966, Nehru's daughter Indira Gandhi was elected the new prime minister. She was popular in part because of her father, but she was not as well loved or as widely trusted as he had been.

Meanwhile, in Pakistan, political trouble was widespread. Since independence, Pakistan had struggled to run a country divided by 1,000 miles of hostile territory.

Jawaharlal Nehru's daughter, Indira Gandhi (left), visits with U.S. first lady Jacqueline Kennedy in March 1962.

Though the capital and most leaders of Pakistan were in West Pakistan, the majority of the people lived in East Pakistan. The East Pakistanis often felt ignored by the government in West Pakistan. The ongoing conflict with India only added to the stress.

The Creation of Bangladesh

In 1971, East Pakistan, tired of being controlled by West Pakistan, decided to break free, and a civil war began. The war was motivated partly by a series of natural disasters that had killed hundreds of thousands of people. The people of East Pakistan thought that West Pakistan had ignored their emergency needs. As the brutal fighting spread, millions of East Pakistanis fled into India, and India became directly involved. At first, India attacked both East and West Pakistan. Then, in December 1971, India allowed the people of East Pakistan to declare themselves the independent nation of Bangladesh, and immediately agreed to support Bangladesh against Pakistan. Together, India and Bangladesh were defeating Pakistan when the UN once again arranged a cease-fire. After this third undeclared war, India and Pakistan entered a period of better relations. They signed a peace treaty and a trade accord, and agreed to respect the boundary line of Kashmir.

Domestic Political Affairs

The next 20 years were relatively peaceful, though both India and Pakistan faced many internal problems. Indira Gandhi was forced to resign from office in 1977, because many Indians thought she had abused her power and tried to keep her political enemies from threatening her rule. Her elected successor was no more popular, however, and she was reelected in 1980. She faced a crisis when followers of the Sikh religion began to try to make the Punjab independent from India. These separatists were responsible for a series of bombings, and Gandhi ordered an invasion of the Sikhs' Golden Temple in Amritsar. Soon after, Gandhi's own bodyguards, who were Sikhs, assassinated her for violating their sacred space. Rajiv Gandhi, Indira's son, was elected prime minister after her death in 1984. He was voted out in 1989, but was seeking re-election in 1991 when he, too, was assassinated.

Pakistan, meanwhile, had its own political problems. After its constitution was finally put in place, the nation was led by a series of elected politicians who were accused of corruption. Through the conflicts with India and the years without a constitution, Pakistan's military had become very influential. When Prime Minister Zulfikar Ali Bhutto was charged with corruption in 1977, the military seized control of the government and executed him. General Muhammad Zia-ul-Haq took over the government and named himself president in 1978, though he promised to restore democracy. After ten years, Zia was killed in a plane crash, and the military leaders agreed to allow new elections.

Bhutto's daughter, Benazir, was elected prime minister in 1988—the first woman to lead an Islamic nation. Two years later, she was dismissed on charges of corruption, and Nawaz Sharif was elected. Still, Bhutto remained popular with the Pakistani people. Many believed she had been removed mainly for political reasons. Reelected in 1993, Bhutto served three more years before she was once again forced from office for corruption. When she ran again in 1997, she was defeated.

Benazir Bhutto was the first woman prime minister of Pakistan.

THE SIKHS

Around A.D. 1500, a Hindu man named Nanak believed that he received enlightenment from God (whom he called Wahegru), which led him to start a new religion. Nanak lived in an area that is now in the Indian state of the Punjab, south of Kashmir, along the border between India and Pakistan. Then, as now, that region was a place where Hindus and Muslims often clashed over politics and religion.

Nanak became known as a guru, or one who brings enlightenment. His new religion was called Sikhism. It blended several of the conflicting ideas of Islam and Hinduism, although Sikhs consider it a completely independent faith. Like Islam, Sikhism accepts only one God, forbids the worship of any images, and does not follow a caste system. Sikhs do, however, believe in the Hindu concept of reincarnation.

The Punjab city of Amritsar became the holy city for the Sikhs, and since the late sixteenth century, the Golden Temple there has been their holiest temple. At Sikhism's founding, neither Hindus nor Muslims acknowledged it as a separate religion, and both groups frequently attacked the Sikhs to bring them back "under control." These attacks led the Sikhs to develop their own strong military, and training with weapons from a young age became part of Sikh culture.

Sikh men take the word Singh, or "lion," as part of their name. Sikh women take Kaur, or "princess." Sikhs are expected to wear the "five K's:" uncut hair, a comb, a steel bracelet, a short sword, and undershorts. (The names of these items all start with K in the Sikh language, Punjabi.) Today, the items symbolize a Sikh's devotion, but originally they were military aids. The hair and comb acted as an extra helmet, the bracelet could be a partial shield, the sword was for defense, and the shorts helped enable freedom of movement.

Sikhs do not cut their hair as a symbol of their devotion to God.

Over time, the Sikhs developed such a reputation for military talent that they were often hired as bodyguards for India's upper class. This is why Indira Gandhi had Sikh bodyguards while she was prime minister. After she ordered the invasion of the Golden Temple in 1984, her Sikh bodyguards killed her—to defend their land and religion as Sikhs had done for centuries.

Religious Tensions Continue

Relations between the governments of India and Pakistan remained generally stable for several years, but by the 1990s, there was cause for concern. Periodic violence between Hindus and Muslims within India was not uncommon. In 1992, for example, Hindu extremists destroyed a sixteenth-century mosque, which led to nationwide riots by India's Muslims. In 1993, 800 Hindus and Muslims died in a series of religious riots in Bombay. Hindu extremists formed a nationalist political party, called the Bharatiya Janata Party, or BJP. Members of this party wanted to take back disputed land such as Kashmir and parts of India's northwest border. They opposed the spread of Islam, as well as any other non-Hindu religions, and attacked Christian churches and schools as well as Islamic mosques.

In 1998, the BJP won the national election for parliament, and the party's leader, Atal Behari Vajpayee, became India's prime minister. Although Vajpayee is considered more moderate than many other Hindu nationalists, his election made India's Muslims fear that the attacks on mosques would continue.

The BJP was also strongly opposed to Pakistan's control over Azad Kashmir, and tensions along that border increased quickly. Later in 1998, both India and Pakistan tested

India's prime minister, Atal Behari Vajpayee, belonged to the Bharatiya Janata Party, which strongly opposed Pakistan's control of Kashmir.

nuclear weapons in an act each nation intended to be a clear warning to the other. In 1999, Indian troops entered Kashmir to attack Muslim rebels who were responsible for a series of bombings. Pakistan sent its military to the border, and both countries sent small forces and artillery across the border at different points. Although the clash did not turn into a full-scale war, the two nations' possession of nuclear

General Pervez Musharraf named himself Pakistan's president in 2001.

weapons made this confrontation more dangerous than any in their past.

In the middle of this conflict, Pakistan's prime minister, Sharif, tried to remove powerful Pakistani general Pervez Musharraf and replace him with someone more loyal to Sharif. Instead, Musharraf and the army overthrew Sharif and reestablished military rule over Pakistan. Many Pakistani people, fearful of the BJP in India and the renewed battle in Kashmir, welcomed Musharraf as a protector. In 2001, Musharraf named himself president of Pakistan, but promised that Pakistan would soon return to open democracy.

CHAPTER THREE

The Future

Life in southern Asia remains a challenge for many people. India has the world's second largest population, and although its economy is the fifth largest in the world, many of its people live in poverty. India is home to several of the world's largest cities, but less than one-third of the population lives in them; agriculture in rural areas still provides jobs for two-thirds of the workforce. India's often overcrowded cities have sections plagued by terrible poverty not far from areas of great wealth. Pollution and disease are major issues in most of India's population centers.

India also faces difficulties in several other areas. Some of India's states have tried actively to gain independence. Kashmir is the best known of these, but even if India allowed Kashmir to break away (which could help end the feud with Pakistan), it would worry that other states, including the Punjab and West Bengal, might try to do the same.

Many people in India are not in a position to worry about politics; almost 40 percent of the population lives below the poverty level, and almost half cannot read or write. Health conditions are also a major concern. More than 3.5 million people in India have HIV or AIDS; tuberculosis, polio, malaria, cholera, and health problems related to pollution

---

Poverty is a huge problem in Pakistan. Some Pakistanis must search through garbage to look for anything that could be useful.

Peace demonstrations were held at the India-Pakistan border in 2001. This man's shirt bears the flags of both India (on left) and Pakistan.

are all found in regions throughout India.

Pakistan faces some hardships similar to those in India, and fewer people and a smaller economy mean it has fewer resources to meet those challenges. In Pakistan, under 40 percent of all people can read; fewer than 30 percent of women can read. Also, political instability has not allowed the economy to grow much, and Pakistan still relies heavily on agriculture. As in India, about 40 percent of the people live in poverty. Although AIDS is not as great a crisis in Pakistan as it is in India, tuberculosis, polio, and malaria are all health threats. Surrounded by often hostile neighbors, including India and Afghanistan, Pakistan has had to spend a great deal of money to keep its armed forces strong. Pakistan has the eighth largest military in the world, and events in 2001 showed the need for this force.

The War on Terrorism

The events that took place on September 11, 2001, changed the relationships among several countries in southern Asia. Al Qaeda, a terrorist organization, launched an attack on the United States that destroyed New York City's World Trade Center and damaged the Pentagon in Washington, D.C. When the government of Afghanistan was condemned for its support of al Qaeda and other terrorist groups, the United States decided to remove the Afghan government (called the Taliban) and destroy the nation's terrorist bases. Pakistan shares a long border with Afghanistan. As a result, when the United States asked Pakistan for assistance, the war against Afghanistan began to affect both Pakistan and India.

U.S. relations with Pakistan have varied since 1947. For the most part, the United States has supported Pakistan with both money and weapons, although that aid was cut off several times in response to U.S. concerns about Pakistan's development of nuclear weapons. Throughout much of the Cold War between the United States and the Soviet Union, from 1945 to 1991, India tried to stay neutral, and the United States saw Pakistan as an important ally. When Soviet troops invaded Afghanistan in 1979, the United States greatly increased aid to support both Pakistan and the Afghan fighters who opposed the Soviets. Pakistan's involvement was a crucial part of the process that eventually led to the removal of Soviet troops from Afghanistan in 1988.

In 1991, the Soviet Union fell. This meant that the United States no longer had to reward Pakistan for its opposition to the Soviet Union. Instead, the

MOTHER TERESA

One woman became world famous for her willingness to fight disease, poverty, and injustice in India. Gonxha Bojaxhiu was born to Albanian parents in Macedonia in 1910. When she was 18, she joined a Catholic order and was given the name Sister Teresa. The next year, the order sent her to Calcutta to teach in a Catholic school. In Calcutta, she took her final vows as a nun.

Sister Teresa believed that in 1946, she received a new calling from God that instructed her to serve the "poorest of the poor." She got permission to move into Calcutta's slums, and started a school for poor children. They called her Mother Teresa. To help in her work, she started an order called the Missionaries of Charity in 1950. In 1952, she founded Nirmal Hriday, or "Pure Heart," a home for the dying in Calcutta. This home was designed to give comfort and dignity to terminally ill people who could not afford housing or care. The next year, she started her first orphanage. She worked with people afflicted with all kinds of diseases, including AIDS, leprosy, cholera, and tuberculosis.

Mother Teresa won many prizes and awards through her lifetime, including the Nobel Peace Prize in 1979 and the United States Medal of Freedom in 1985. Her Missionaries of Charity spread to more than 90 nations, and now employs more than 4,000 nuns. When she first tried to retire in 1990, she was voted back into service by the nuns of her order—the only vote against her leadership was her own. She was finally allowed to retire in 1996, after several years of serious illnesses and injuries. She died the next year. There is a strong demand to have the Roman Catholic Church name her a saint for her work with the poor and dying. Mother Teresa's love and work gave hope and peace to millions.

Mother Teresa won the Nobel Peace Prize in 1979.

United States began to increase its support of India, which has a much larger population, and thus, a bigger market for U.S. goods. After the September 11 attacks, however, the United States turned to Pakistan once again. To regain American favor, Musharraf decided to allow the United States to use Pakistan as a base of operations against Afghanistan and the Taliban, and Pakistan became a major partner in the war on terrorism. Many people in Pakistan resisted Musharraf's decision, either because they favored the Taliban or resented U.S. interference in Islamic and regional affairs. Although the increased U.S. aid to Pakistan did not result in a decreased amount of aid to India, it did help insure that the United States would not favor India over Pakistan. With both sides looking for support in the ongoing conflict in Kashmir, that balance is important.

The Conflict Goes On

The continuing conflict between India and Pakistan remains a matter of great concern to the rest of the world. The centuries-long hostility between southern Asia's Muslims and Hindus, combined with the fact that two of the world's largest militaries share a long, disputed border, is frightening. Since both nations have admitted that they possess nuclear weapons, the situation has become even more dangerous. In addition, India's Hindu nationalists and Pakistan's military are known for their resistance to each other, and those are the groups represented by the nations' current leaders. Kashmir sits as a potential spark between them, ready to ignite a war that could affect the rest of the world and perhaps kill millions. In a region that has been home to some of the world's greatest voices for peace, from Buddha to Gandhi to Mother Teresa, the call of war today remains very loud.

The Indian Border Security Force patrols the border between Pakistan and India.

Important Dates

c. 3000 B.C.   Harappan civilization thrives in Indus Valley.

563 B.C.   Birth of Siddhartha Gautama, also known as Buddha.

A.D. 711   Muslim invasions begin in present-day Pakistan.

1001   Mahmud of Ghazni invades northern India and destroys Hindu sites.

1206   Delhi Sultanate begins.

1498   Vasco da Gama lands in India.

1525   Babur invades India and begins Mogul Dynasty.

1556   Rule of Akbar begins; height of Hindu-Muslim cooperation.

1612   British establish trading post in India.

1628   Rule of Shah Jahan begins; Taj Mahal and other remarkable structures built.

1757   British defeat French and control European trade in India.

1853   British build first Indian railway.

1857   Sepoy Mutiny begins; British government takes over rule in India directly.

1885   Indian National Congress formed.

1906   All-India Muslim League founded.

1919   Amritsar Massacre.

1920   Mohandas Gandhi begins public campaign of civil disobedience.

India's Taj Mahal was built in 1628.

1947	India partitioned into India and Pakistan and made independent; mass migrations and war over Kashmir begin.
1948	Gandhi assassinated; Muhammad Ali Jinnah of Pakistan dies.
1964	Jawaharlal Nehru dies.
1965	War between India and Pakistan over Kashmir.
1966	Indira Gandhi becomes India's prime minister.
1971	Civil war between East and West Pakistan; India intervenes on side of East Pakistan, which becomes Bangladesh.
1973	Zulfikar Ali Bhutto becomes prime minister of Pakistan.
1977	Bhutto and Indira Gandhi both removed.
1980	United States supports Pakistan's aid to Afghan resistance fighters against Soviet Union; Indira Gandhi reelected prime minister in India.
1984	Gandhi orders troops to storm Sikhs' Golden Temple in Amritsar; later that year, her Sikh bodyguards assassinate her.
1988	Benazir Bhutto becomes prime minister in Pakistan.
1990	Bhutto removed for corruption; replaced by Nawaz Sharif.
1991	Rajiv Gandhi assassinated.
1992	Hindu nationalists destroy a Muslim mosque in Ayodhya, India.
1993	Muslim-Hindu rioting in Bombay kills 800; Benazir Bhutto reelected in Pakistan.
1996	Bhutto removed again for corruption.
1998	BJP (Hindu nationalist party) and Atal Behari Vajpayee win election; India and Pakistan conduct nuclear tests.
1999	Fighting begins again in Kashmir; Nawaz Sharif overthrown in Pakistan by general Pervez Musharraf.
2001	Pakistan agrees to aid United States in fight against Taliban in Afghanistan.

For More Information

WEBSITES

http://alfa.nic.in/	Official website of India (Parliament).
http://jammukashmir.nic.in/	Official website of Jammu and Kashmir state.
www.bangladeshgov.org/	Official website of Bangladesh.
www.geographia.com/india	Geographia.com's site on Indian history.
www.himalayanacademy.com/	Hinduism online website; history and instruction.
www.hindu.org/	Website with information about Hinduism (history and practice).
www.historyofindia.com	Comprehensive history site broken into key eras.
www.indiaspace.com/quotes.htm	M. K. Gandhi Institute website of Gandhi quotes.
www.nuclearfiles.org/data/	Information on nuclear weapons and nations.
www.pak.gov.pk/	Official website of Pakistan.
www.state.gov/r/pa/ei/bgn/	U.S. State Department background notes on nations; statistics and descriptions.
www.tisv.be/mt/indmt.htm	Mother Teresa official website.

BOOKS

Exploration into India, by Anita Ganeri (Chelsea House, 2000).
Gandhi: Great Soul, by John Severance (Houghton Mifflin, 1997).
India, by Elaine Landau (Childrens Press, 2000).
India: The People, by Bobbie Kalman (Crabtree Publishers, 2000).
Mohandas Gandhi, by Christopher Martin (Lerner Publications, 2000).
Pakistan, by John C. Caldwell (Chelsea House, 1999).

Source Quotations

1. Quoted on-line at http://www.quotesandsayings.com/gindia.htm; accessed September 2002.

2. Quoted on-line in Quotes from Indian History, http://www.geocities.com/glorybangla/iqtes.htm; accessed September 2002.

3. Quoted in *Ganashakti Newsmagazine*, "The Jalianwala Bagh Massacre," on-line at http://www.ganashakti.com/old/1999/990419/feature.htm; accessed September 2002.

4. Quoted on-line at Nonviolence.org, http://www.nonviolence.org/commentary/105.php; accessed November 27, 2002.

5. Quoted from a speech at the Frontier Muslim League Conference, November 21, 1945. On-line in Why Pakistan, http://www.icgt.org/MonitorPastArticles/WhyPakistan.htm; accessed September 2002.

6. Quoted on-line at http://www.dadalos.org/int/Vorbilder/vorbilder/gandhi/Zitate; accessed September 2002.

About the Author

Chris Hughes holds a B.A. in history from Lafayette College and an M.A. in social studies education from Lehigh University. A history teacher and school administrator, Hughes teaches both U.S. and world history and has written several books on the American Civil War and on developing nations. Hughes currently lives and works at a boarding school in Chatham, Virginia, with his wife, Farida, and their children, Jordan and Leah.

Index